Ideas
into
Action

CCL's Research and Innovation Journey

JEAN BRITTAIN LESLIE

WITH PETER L. SCISCO

**Center for
Creative
Leadership**

1 Leadership Place, Greensboro, NC 27410
©2024 Center for Creative Leadership

Published 2024
978-1-64761-114-9 (paperback)
978-1-64761-115-6 (epub)
978-1-64761-116-3 (epdf)
CCL No. 2506

Cataloging in Publication data on file with the Library of Congress.

Table of Contents

Executive Summary   *v*

Acknowledgments   *ix*

Introduction   *xi*

Origins   1

Pioneering Contributions and Founding Philosophy   5

Research Advances   17

Leadership Challenges   37

The Boldness of Uncertain Potentialities   43

Still a Beginning   49

Chronological List of Sources   *51*

About the Authors   *61*

About the Center for Creative Leadership   *63*

Executive Summary

This history of research and innovation at the Center for Creative Leadership (CCL)® traces an often groundbreaking path through the leadership development field. Our mission is to advance the understanding, practice, and development of leadership for the benefit of society worldwide. With funding from the H. Smith Richardson Foundation, we began as a set of connected ideas: to investigate why some businesses sustained themselves while others faltered, how to develop creative leaders, and how to leverage "cross country" thinking. The Foundation provided seed money to support our research on leadership, talent selection and development, and creativity.

From those beginnings, we expanded to campuses and offices around the world. Our emphasis on integrating research with practice and sharing knowledge and ideas has been a guiding principle. It's a constant revisiting of H. Smith Richardson's vision: "It takes boldness to invest in programs of uncertain potentialities, but it's out of such support that some of the greatest discoveries have been made."

The Lessons of Experience (LOE) research we conducted in the early 1980s was groundbreaking in its recognition of the critical link between on-the-job learning and leadership development. It significantly impacted how organizations and leaders think about leadership and how to develop it in a strategic capacity. It was a first step toward the view of leadership as a collective achievement; a perspective that helped us research the dynamics of organizational change and transformation in new ways.

LOE research also had a significant impact on our focus on gender diversity in leadership. Early on, we examined the underrepresentation of women in top leadership roles and identified the root causes. We popularized the term "glass ceiling," and our landmark 1987 book, *Breaking the Glass Ceiling*, continues to influence how organizations manage the opportunities for women seeking leadership roles. LOE research influences our work on equity, diversity, and inclusion.

Because we were focused on developing leaders, we turned our sights on the learning process itself. We codified how leaders can identify their learning preferences, enabling them to purposefully leverage on-the-job learning opportunities and gain insights from their experiences. That development revolutionized the understanding of leadership development by emphasizing the importance of on-the-job learning, the development of broader perspectives, the causes and costs of derailment, and the collective nature of leadership.

We've also contributed to the recognition that leaders aren't found only in formal organizations. Leader and leadership development spans from childhood to adulthood, across geographic and cultural divides and diverse social groups. That perspective is foundational to our vision as the leading force in leadership, expanding human potential to create a better future for the world.

We don't just study leadership and educate leaders about its practice; we also measure the impact of development to ensure that leaders learn and generate ideas, tactics, and strategies that work. Our evaluation efforts cover corporate, government, nonprofit, and educational sectors worldwide. We've blazed a trail in assessing the societal impact of development activities, and we've probed new areas, such as specialized leadership solutions for neurodivergent leaders.

Our founders were interested in the relationship between creativity and leadership, and our work often reflects that interest. From our annual Creativity Weeks in the 1970s and the formation of the Association for Managers of Innovation in 1981 to the design-thinking approaches that informed our Global Voice of Leadership, we've demonstrated that creativity and innovation are manageable processes, not random or hard-to-replicate inspirations.

Another area of keen interest since early in our history is the diverse populations that form workforces and the leadership that serves them. Around the world, our researchers have gathered information and insights on racial, religious, gender, ethnic, and cultural diversity and their effects on learning and on defining experiences. Our research and practice create insights into leading complex, multicultural environments.

As views of leadership changed from individual talents to distributed and collective leadership, we've integrated various streams of its research to yield a possible transformational path for organizations, emphasizing a shift from command and control (dependent) to mutual influence (independent) and ultimately collective activity (interdependent). Our frameworks and tools facilitate robust organizational leadership development alongside individual leader development.

We also emphasize the significance of collaborative, high-performing teams in organizations. We diagnose team strengths and connections, particularly within senior leadership teams. We include virtual and hybrid teams within our work with traditional teams and those dispersed around the word. Our research provides insights and practices for fostering skilled, agile, and networked teams capable of efficient collaboration.

We have also developed new perspectives on the inner lives of leaders. We look at leadership wellbeing and resilience, for example. We investigate cognitive distortions, emotion regulation, stress, and other factors in a holistic approach to leadership development. Using self-tracking wearables and sensor-enabled technology, we've revealed opportunities for leaders to develop continuously, independent of experts or coaches. We've also used artificial intelligence (AI) algorithms to analyze challenges to, and responses from, leaders. By encompassing life experiences, well-being, and personal development, we've expanded the definition of "leadership readiness."

We recognize the unique challenges faced by top-level executives and their need for accurate developmental feedback, even as we acknowledge that first-time managers have specific challenges of their own. Programs like Maximizing Your Leadership Potential and our Leadership Challenge Ladder project highlight valuable developmental insights and guide organizations in designing efficient development strategies for leaders at all levels of their operations.

Change management is another critical aspect of our work. We investigate and communicate practical wisdom about the emotional and cultural aspects of change, which often doom systemic-level change efforts.

CCL's adaptability and commitment to enriching the understanding of leadership in the contemporary world make us a pivotal contributor to leadership development in the 21st century. As we look to the future, we remain committed to the pursuit of knowledge. Our research teams, characterized by their radical diversity, ensure that our research stays relevant to leaders and organizations around the world. We continue our mission by seeking to expand human potential, and to help leaders develop the mindsets, capacity, and capabilities needed to excel in an ever-changing world. CCL's leadership development work, backed by research and fueled by our pursuit of innovation and impact, guides us to make a transformative impact on individuals, organizations, and communities worldwide.

Acknowledgments

S pecial acknowledgments go to Sarah Glover and Meena Wilson for developing an earlier edition of this work in 2006 under the title *Unconventional Wisdom*. It's the cornerstone on which this revised edition stands. In the years that followed, scores of researchers, trainers, collaborators, and partners have added their stories to our tale of exploration, inquiry, validation, and practical wisdom. For those sources especially relevant to this book, we have arranged them in chronological order to show the trajectory of CCL's intellectual and practical history. Special thanks to David Altman for his support, and to Anand Chandrasekar, John Fleenor, Laura Gibson, Cynthia McCauley, John McGuire, Chuck Palus, Marian Ruderman, Sarah Stawiski, and Ellen Van Velsor for their feedback on earlier versions. All of them, and many others, share the success of this work.

Introduction

Since the founding of CCL in 1970, our commitment to research and innovation has been central to fulfilling our mission: To advance the understanding, practice, and development of leadership for the benefit of society worldwide — and that commitment remains as strong as ever. This book describes some of CCL's most important work in research and innovation and sets the stage for future innovation and developments.

Our research agenda began as a question, as research often does. Generally, it was a question of organizational sustainability; specifically, a question about the role of leadership in that achievement. If skillful leadership affects the longevity and the relevance of an organization, what kind of leaders possess that skill, and how can it be developed and practiced? Further, if skillful leadership produces positive, longstanding effects in commercial organizations, can it do the same outside of the world of business? And if organizations pursue a leadership developmental strategy, how will they know if it has had an impact? Seeking answers to such questions drives much of our research and innovation efforts.

From our start as a small group of researchers and classroom trainers to our current global footprint, we remain dedicated to the vision of our founders and our mission. As CCL looks to the future, our vision is to be the leading force in leadership, expanding human potential to create a better future for the world. In 2024, our pursuit of understanding leadership and how it can develop still generates questions, and the evidence arising from those inquiries creates practical insight in unexpected and fruitful ways.

Origins

Early in the 20th century in Greensboro, North Carolina (USA), Lunsford Richardson, with the help of his son H. Smith Richardson, founded a company to sell and distribute a series of home remedies he had invented as a small-town pharmacist. The son urged that the company focus its effort on a single product: a salve called Vicks® VapoRub™, which contained menthol and was sold as relief for head and chest congestion. By 1929, Vicks® VapoRub™ was sold around the world, and eventually, the family business grew into the Vick Chemical Company.

What was behind that success? H. Smith Richardson thought a lot about the sustainability of family firms, observing that new leaders in such circumstances often fail after taking over from the previous generation. Out of his concern and general interest in what successful leadership is, what it accomplishes, and how it's developed, The Smith Richardson Foundation was born in 1935, funding scholars and behavioral scientists to study topics related to leadership and creativity. Such research sustained the vitality of the family business, and in 1957, H. Smith Richardson, Jr. became the next generation to successfully lead the worldwide organization.

While Richardson Sr. was fascinated with creativity and innovation, his son was convinced that selection, development, and utilization of talent were equally critical to sustaining organizations. Richardson Jr. believed this field of study would be better served if it was the focus of a separate entity charged with finding ways to select, develop, and utilize creative leadership to connect the findings of research to practical purposes in the business arena. It would take existing tools, perfect them, and make them available for the betterment of all leaders.

In 1970, that entity — the Center for Creative Leadership® — was founded. Our purpose was to expand those initial queries into creativity, innovation, talent, and development. We fashioned ourselves to meet the needs of individual leaders, businesses, and, ultimately, all organizations. Since then, we've successfully combined a sustained investment in leadership research with an educational purpose. Our emphasis on integrating research and practice and broadly sharing that knowledge are important parts of our ethos and remain a guiding principle, embodied in a rallying slogan, "ideas into action." Complementing that phrase is an equally important commitment: "action into ideas."

Over subsequent decades, we've extended our mission worldwide, opening a second US-based campus in Colorado Springs, Colorado in 1983, followed by a third in San Diego, California in 1987. We began working in India during the 1980s, and officially incorporated an office there in 2009. We created a European presence in 1990 when we opened an office in Brussels, Belgium. In 2003, we entered the Asia-Pacific region with a Singapore campus designed to serve leaders in that sphere, and established a Gurgaon, India office in 2009.

In 2012, we strengthened our presence in Europe, the Middle East, and Africa by transforming our Brussels office into a regional headquarters and training campus. One year later, we opened a Shanghai office. Additional Middle East and Africa locations followed in Addis Ababa, Ethiopia in 2006; Moscow in 2008; Johannesburg, South Africa in 2012; Dubai, UAE in 2022; and Saudi Arabia in 2023.

While we now span 4 continents, our origin story is always close at hand; a reminder of the energy that created our mission. The name itself — Center for Creative Leadership — is bound to H. Smith Richardson's vision and philosophy. All those years ago, he believed that leadership required creative responses to change to avoid or overcome the usual pitfalls and unforeseen challenges of leading an organization toward sustainability capable of renewing itself over time.

A quote from H. Smith Richardson, found on the walls of our Greensboro, NC headquarters, remains a vital statement of the ideas that launched CCL and continues to influence our research agenda today: "It takes boldness to invest in programs of uncertain potentialities, but it is out of such support that some of the greatest discoveries have been made."

Pioneering Contributions and Founding Philosophy

At CCL's founding, leadership development was a novel concept. A common adage of that era was "leaders are born, not made." We instead proposed the radical notion (at that time) that leadership can be learned. That belief led to new fields of research and a new industry: management and leadership development.

Assessment for Development: A Bold Idea

Having accepted that leaders can be developed, we wanted to know how that growth happens. Our research started with a couple of hypotheses that evolved into guiding principles: (1) leader development is synonymous with personal development, and (2) the key to professional and personal growth is "assessment for development." Our research showed that leaders learn and change most when they become self-aware of their current state, take on a challenge that stretches their abilities, and have support that helps them meet that challenge. We captured that perspective in our framework for development: Assessment – Challenge – Support (ACS)™. Development can and does occur without all those elements, but with less impact. The elements of ACS are found in our practice of feedback, in our group exercises, and in the safe environment created by our classroom facilitators and coaches. We described the framework and its implications in the 1998 edition of *The Center for Creative Leadership Handbook of Leadership Development.*

The concept of assessment for development was as radical as insisting that leaders were made, not born. Assessment for selection, promotion, or performance review were the established aims of assessment in the 1970s. In breaking new ground, we found two features of assessment for development to be most important: (1) it would provide assessment data (feedback) to the person being assessed, contrary to the established practice at the time of giving assessment data to the person's boss; and (2) it would maintain the confidentiality of the data so that the person assessed has control over how it's used and shared.

By following these two principles, we create a safe psychological space where managers and leaders can more easily accept the feedback they receive from others. Further, the feedback itself is more honest because the people giving it do so anonymously. This approach to assessment for development forms the cornerstone of our work.

We also believe that leadership development works at all levels in organizations because it's consistent with personal development, which follows the natural human path of learning from experience. As we researched and practiced leader development, the beneficial impact of ACS suggested that developmental activities on the job or elsewhere could be designed with ACS in mind. Our framework — along with its assessment-for-development practice and its knowledge of the social and psychological factors in human development — applies to senior leadership teams, first-time managers, community leaders, students, and educators, in both profit and nonprofit organizations.

Building a Learning Laboratory

To validate our beliefs about leadership and leadership development, we needed access to real-life, practicing leaders and managers as opposed to university students who at the time were commonly used as subjects for academic research. By 1974, we decided to assess our theories about leadership, creativity, and experiential education by building a program using techniques we had been studying: the Leadership Development Program (LDP)®. Inviting practicing leaders to participate in that program gave us an accessible laboratory from which to observe and learn skillful leadership. Today, LDP remains our flagship program. Tens of thousands of leaders worldwide have used the program to develop the skills and capacities required to guide themselves, their teams, and their organizations toward sustained success.

Around the same time that we created LDP, a small team of CCL researchers interested in how managers share information and make decisions built a simulation that replicated a day in a manager's work life. The goal of the project was pure research: Build a simulation, run managers through it, observe them, and then collect and analyze the data. In terms of design and methods, we built off the work of Henry Mintzberg, one of the leading scholars in what was then the infant science of business theory and management. We introduced our simulation, Looking Glass, Inc.® (LGI), in 1979.

Simply collecting and analyzing data, while valuable to researchers, was insufficient for the managers participating in LGI. They wanted feedback on the quality of their performance in the simulation, and we used this opportunity to further our work on assessment for development. In shifting our focus from data collection to experiential practices (from ideas to action), we built support around the LGI simulation to help managers learn from their experiences during the simulation. We dubbed the simulation and supporting interactions "The Looking Glass Experience," or "LGE," in 1978. Thousands of managers have tried their hand at running this simulated glass manufacturing company, either by attending the simulation at a CCL campus or by attending licensed versions facilitated by our network of providers.

The LGI simulation continues to evolve. In one team research project, for example, we investigated how behaviors (as part of a group's dynamics) relate to a team's input, processes, and outcomes. Within the Looking

Glass® simulation, researchers use a range of technologies to observe speaking time, turn-taking, questions, and interruptions. The data being collected is shared with the participants during the simulation — an example of real-time sharing of research-based insights.

Around this time, we also developed the "Leader Development Roadmap." It was designed to help people interested in attending a CCL class select the developmental experience that matched their needs. (For example, the manager of a business unit would have different needs, developmentally, than a first-time manager). It also helped leaders envision the developmental path they might take. The combination of LGE with the roadmap was codified as "Leading for Organizational Impact."

Pioneering 360-Degree Assessment

At first, we used only self-report assessments; however, in the mid-1970s, we began the development of a "multisource feedback" survey. The value of using the ratings of others as an assessment of leadership in our programs became immediately apparent. In 1978, we published *Feedback to Managers: A Comprehensive Review of Twenty-Four Instruments*, which reviewed existing leadership assessments available at that time (the book was revised in 1991 and again in 2013.) Although the title has been modified over its three editions, this publication remains a crucial guide to the field of managerial assessments. Further, the book represents our forward-looking identification of trends in the field. *Feedback to Managers* is one of many examples of how, even from its earliest days, we took on the role of gathering and integrating research to make practice and theory available to others. However, the broad accessibility of knowledge goes beyond *Feedback to Managers*. Scores of peer-reviewed articles written by our researchers have been developed from CCL's 360-degree assessment (360) data, as well as scholarly dissertations and theses.

A large part of our contribution to the leadership development field in the 1980s was our creation of 360-degree assessment tools designed specifically for leadership development, which involves the full circle of people with whom an employee interacts at work: boss, peers, and direct reports.

We used the term "360-degree feedback" in its 1991 edition of *Feedback to Managers*. The early days of 360-degree feedback are described in the introduction to *The Handbook of Multisource Feedback* (2001).

One of our first 360-degree assessment instruments, Skillscope®, debuted in 1986 as part of LGE. We developed Skillscope so that managers participating in LGE could learn how their actual co-workers saw them. From that perspective, Skillscope measures skills necessary for effectiveness in a management role. Benchmarks®, a multi-rater assessment created to assess leadership strengths and weaknesses, was released in 1988. We described its development in a 1989 *Journal of Management* article, "Diagnosing Management Development Needs." Benchmarks originated from interviews with executives that identified 32 categories of lessons they reported learning during their careers, and 16 items measuring skills and perspectives were created for the Benchmarks instrument after further analysis of those categories.

Our researchers described their early attempts to integrate existing knowledge about 360-degree feedback in a 1993 special issue of *Human Resource Management*. Other publications followed about the research into, and advances made in, the development and use of 360-degree assessments (*Maximizing the Value of 360-degree Feedback* in 1998, for example). We continue to share our ongoing research into 360-degree assessments in publications such as *Leveraging the Impact of 360-degree Feedback* (2008; 2020), a blueprint for implementing 360-degree approaches to development within organizations.

We've created six different 360-degree assessment tools over the years, updating them as new research findings or advancing technology warrant. In addition to Skillscope, they are Benchmarks (1988); Executive Dimensions (2000; later refined and renamed Benchmarks® for Executives™), Prospector (1995; later refined and renamed Benchmarks for Learning Agility™), and Campbell Leadership Indicator (2012). Benchmarks itself was further developed into a customized version in 2001 called 360 By Design. That assessment was built around a library of more than 90 of what we initially called "skills and perspectives," from which leader-development professionals could choose to tailor a 360-degree assessment to suit their organization's leader development needs. The customizable assessment was later refined and renamed Benchmarks by Design™ to highlight the instrument's heritage.

Our pioneering research and validation of 360-degree assessment tools and feedback techniques revolutionized the assessment process and enabled us to build an extensive assessment database. (Currently, we process over 42,000 participant assessments each year.) In *The Benchmarks Sourcebook* (2011, 2023), we surveyed the academic studies of the data generated by that assessment, which is periodically revised to include our most recent research.

No description of our pioneering 360-assessment work would be complete without a critical historical note on the demographics at the heart of our assessment research. At the start of our research work, the pool of subjects was comprised of managers and executives in North American organizations. In the 1970s and 80s, the norms within that general pool, by and large, assumed White American males held management and leadership positions. That norm was reflected in our research at the time because CCL researchers drew from management titles cataloged in the US Bureau of Labor Statistics.

Those norms changed over the years as organizations globalized and diversified. Our research responded to those shifts and, in many instances, anticipated them. Not only did we translate our assessments into multiple languages, but we pioneered the use of psychometric analyses in different cultural contexts to refine skills, perspectives, and items. That groundbreaking work, which began with women and African American leaders, ensured the cultural appropriateness of our assessments and defined measurement equivalence across different language and groups.

Despite the limits of research into a homogeneous population of White, North American males at the start of our investigative work, we marked two key differentiators that affect how people develop as leaders (which carry over across lines of culture, identity, race, gender, and other perceived boundaries): personality and job experiences. Those common differentiators led us toward the position that leadership development could be useful for everyone — an idea that, over time, evolved into a major initiative and a strategic driver to our success today: democratizing leadership.

Leadership Excellence for All

From its earliest days, we've made our work accessible to as many people as possible, in keeping with our mission to work "for the benefit of society worldwide." We've extended our work developing organizational leaders to broader audiences by making our insights, practices, and resources available in books — "toolkits" for facilitating learning, and online. The *Feedback to Managers* books, for example, help leaders choose and assess 360s and can be used as guides, saving organizations and others the time and expense of researching the field themselves.

Our history of ideas can be traced in some of our major book releases: *The Center for Creative Leadership Handbook of Leadership Development* (1998; 2004; 2010); *The CCL Handbook of Coaching* (2006); *The Handbook of Leadership Development Evaluation* (2006); and *The Center for Creative Leadership Handbook of Coaching in Organizations* (2015). Those books share our theory, practice, and philosophy of development, describe how we create experiences for development, and lay out how we evaluate our work to measure its effectiveness. We've also created online access to CCL's research and innovation in 2020, including a beta program for new facilitation and learning toolkits at cclinnovation.org.

Democratizing Leadership

As mentioned above, one of CCL's responses to ongoing change in managerial roles and the people in them was to extend our early LOE research to include women and African American leaders. We also turned our attention to the range of generations working side by side in organizations. These groups and others had certain circumstances and experiences worth incorporating into a perspective on and approach to leadership development.

Our intent from early on was to ensure that leaders have access to developmental opportunities that mirror their experiences in the world. Knowledge and practice about leaders and how they develop must remain relevant and effective to create a beneficial impact. During our years of research and practice, we've produced several landmark publications on leaders from groups traditionally underrepresented in the United States.

Those books included *The New Leaders: Guidelines on Leadership Diversity in America* (1992) and *The New Leaders: Leadership Diversity in America* (1996).

Even with our insight into the leadership potential of a diverse work-force, we realized — as did many others — that most of the people on this planet are young and live in rural areas or densely populated cities with difficult access to education. Most aren't employed by organizations, inter-national or otherwise. What would happen if we brought leadership devel-opment research and practice to under-resourced communities, villages, and hamlets outside the rarefied air of multinational companies or carefully crafted school curriculums? Would our work integrate with beliefs about leadership already held by such disparate communities? Could it enhance those beliefs? Could it learn from them?

We were already addressing generational, geographical, and cultural differences among aspiring leaders, and we'd gained insight into how the ideas and principles of leadership development could play a transformative role outside of formal organizations. To share these insights, we established the Global Voice of Leadership (GVOL). Under that banner, we devised ways of bringing what we had learned about leadership development to commu-nities historically underserved by the field, including young people.

In 1988, we expanded our work into the social sector, establishing a formal group called Education and Nonprofit (ENP). Initially, the group's work in Education was focused on Superintendents of K–12 schools in keep-ing with our approach of serving senior leaders in organizations to create the potential to affect the rest of the organization. Likewise, ENP's work with nonprofit organizations focused on developing the leadership capacity of executive directors.

As ENP evolved, it took advantage of partnerships with foundations that enabled it to extend leadership development beyond the executive director to all levels of the nonprofit organizations. It also expanded from collaborating with superintendents to collaborating with school principals, because principals are critical to improving student and school outcomes.

ENP's work was focused on US organizations, and we looked from there outward. The heart of ENP's mission was to take what it learned about leadership development to communities historically underserved by the field, including young people.

Driven by its vision to democratize leadership development, we developed GVOL further and adopted the name Leadership Beyond Boundaries (LBB). The intent of LBB was to make leadership development affordable, scalable, and accessible to audiences not typically among recipients of leadership development. By conducting immersive research and experiments in India, East Africa, and Eastern Europe, we gained a key insight: We could indeed scale our reach and impact by packaging and sharing our practical knowledge of leadership development with local grassroots organizations present where we were not. (The ideas that shaped democratizing leadership efforts appeared in the 2010 edition of *The Handbook of Leadership Development.*)

At the heart of LBB were simplified curriculums called Leadership Essentials. LBB used those toolkits and train-the-trainer designs in more than 50 countries. That extension of learning embedded leadership development in organizations working on conflict mitigation, public health, women empowerment, youth development, entrepreneurship, agricultural development, governance, and more. In each case, those organizations recognized that social challenges relate to human factors such as empowerment, behavioral change, collaboration, and innovation —things that we knew a lot about.

In addition to service organizations, LBB worked with youth organizations and schools, spanning K–12 to secondary education. As with other organizations, the goal was to embed leadership development into the fabric of education. In 2020, some specific tools and strategies for teachers and other faculty to boost leadership skills among young people were published in *Social-Emotional Leadership: A Guide for Youth Development.* Research with schoolchildren aged 3–12 led to a 2022 book about leadership aimed at kids: *Building Bridges: Leadership for You and Me.*

The ENP and LBB initiatives expanded our impact from tens of thousands to hundreds of thousands of people, without having to build new campuses and employ more trainers and coaches (some of the factors that typically kept leadership development from becoming more affordable and accessible). From those beginnings, the idea of democratizing leadership has developed into an important and fruitful area of our work: Societal Impact. In more than 50 countries, Societal Impact has become an integral part of youth development, K–12 and higher-education leadership development, nonprofit organizations, foundations and philanthropic organizations, and public health. Where GVOL envisioned making leadership development available to the broadest audience possible, ENP and LBB created practices for putting that vision into action. Societal Impact has used those ideas and innovations to truly democratize leadership.

Leadership as a Collective Achievement

The field of leadership development, since its earliest days, has focused on leadership as more or less "what a leader does." In that view, the quality of leadership hinges primarily on the traits, skills, styles, and relationships of individuals and the nature of the environment in which they find themselves. But by the mid-1990s, we realized that traditional approaches toward understanding the nature of leadership and how it might develop were constrained by those views.

Our work progressed to include customized development programs within organizations, to involve senior executive teams and team development generally, and to extend into non-Western societies. It also highlighted assumptions about leadership linked to cultural differences (organizational and societal) and the growing importance of teams as a driver of organizational success. At the same time, other leadership scholars outside of CCL were exploring concepts of shared leadership, distributed leadership, and leadership as an emergent property of systems — alternatives to the idea that individual leaders are the source of leadership.

What might it look like if leadership was developed not as skill-building but as navigating and orchestrating the dynamics of communal activity? If that were the case, how might organizations approach innovation, transformation, and a host of other challenges organizations face but that a collection of individual leadership skills, no matter how finely tuned, often struggle to engage?

The beginnings of a broader way of understanding leadership already existed within CCL. Grounded in relational theory, our 1994 book, *Making Common Sense: Leadership as Meaning-Making in a Community of Practice*, argued that leadership is emergent and contextual, located in the interactions and exchanges within groups of people with shared work. These ideas were further developed in *The Deep Blue Sea: Rethinking the Source of Leadership* (2001). We began to see leadership as a collective achievement rather than simply the actions of influential individuals. That shift in perspective stimulated the development of dialogue tools, such as *Visual Explorer* in 2014, and it opened the way toward understanding the power of organizational culture.

Research Advances

By recognizing that experience is key to development, CCL continued research into evaluating the effectiveness of developmental experiences and put forth practical approaches for bridging the differences between cultures, races, ethnicities, and geographies. New and influential perspectives on the nature of leadership, organizational culture, and change broadened our understanding of what could be achieved with skilled leadership. Fieldwork with underserved populations established leadership development more equitably and broadly so it could benefit society worldwide. What follows is a chronological summary of some of our major research advances in leadership development.

Lessons of Experience

In the early 1980s, our researchers collaborated with learning and development executives in major organizations on a series of studies to pinpoint what sparked learning, growth, and change in managers. They named this research stream Lessons of Experience (LOE). In designing and implementing LOE, we were among the first leadership-development organizations to recognize and emphasize the critical link between on-the-job learning and leadership development.

At the time, many in leadership development assumed that managers learn from educational experiences, their job experiences, and important people in their lives. Our research showed that challenging job assignments make up the largest part of what managers say they learn from; that bosses, good or bad, were the most common category of people that they said they learned from (not mentors or coaches), and that they learned from hardships, not only successes. The research also explained that different patterns of lessons could be learned from different types of experiences.

Bigger Minds

The early results of LOE were first published in *Key Events in Executives' Lives* in 1987, which described four situations from which managers learn the skills of leadership: challenging assignments, hardships, professional relationships, and other less obvious but nonetheless important areas of development. The bestselling book *The Lessons of Experience* (1988) followed and contributed significantly to research and practice in the human resources field. The LOE findings have been replicated by researchers in universities and in regions around the world, and we've found more similarities than differences in developmental experiences across countries, industries, and organizations.

One of the most far-reaching insights from LOE was that managers didn't just develop skills from their experience; they also developed broader perspectives and more sophisticated ways of making sense of the world. That powerful insight generated a rich vein of research and practice that created entirely new ways of defining leadership at CCL — it was the kernel to the ideas described in this book's connected leadership section, and it opened the door to thinking of leadership as a collective endeavor. The revelation of developing broader perspectives revealed new insights in the context of organizational culture change. Developing leaders expanded the vantage point from which they could analyze shifting organizational situations. For example, in the case of what we called "vertical leadership culture," CCL modeled a trajectory of development from independent (individual leaders) to dependent (independent groups) to interdependent (fully relational awareness between individuals, groups, and the organization, expressed through its culture).

The consequences of this insight eventually influenced our change and transformation work (among other things). In a 2017 paper, we showed how leaders wishing to change their organizational cultures must first gauge where their culture is in the hierarchy of cultures, and then understand the capabilities needed for their future business strategy to succeed. In some cases, the authors argue, leaders must "slow down to power up" to lead change.

Developing Women Leaders

When we employed our LOE interview techniques in CCL's Executive Women Project, it highlighted female underrepresentation in top leadership roles. That original research explained the root causes of the phenomenon and provided data and recommendations to accelerate change. The impact is still felt today.

That work also helped popularize the memorable "glass ceiling" metaphor to describe the invisible obstacles women encounter trying to advance in management. The landmark book *Breaking the Glass Ceiling* (1987) put us at the forefront of understanding barriers facing women leaders, inspiring decades of further research and publicizing key issues affecting women seeking leadership roles in organizations: What does it take for women to enter the executive suite? What factors advance women toward top positions? What knocks them off track? Do women need the same opportunities for development as men?

Learning to Learn

To explain the process of development so that leaders could benefit from a sharper awareness regarding the inherent stress that comes with learning new skills and perspectives (the "challenge" part of ACS), we mapped the "anatomy" of learning in *Learning How to Learn from Experience* in 1992. In one of those serendipitous paths that thread through our history, the tension between learning from experience and stress prompted an insight into how different leaders learn from their experiences in different ways, and that insight created *The Learning Tactics Inventory* (LTI) in 1992. The LTI helps managers better understand their learning preferences so they can become more purposeful about learning from on-the-job opportunities and experience in general.

Experience-Based Development

After the importance of developmental experiences became clear, one of the next questions was how organizations and individual leaders might embed those experiences in a strategy of learning. The answer (or answers) depends on understanding how development occurs: Is it the "aha moment" of insight or the accretion of skill and knowledge over time? And if it's both, how do they relate within a process of learning?

Development Is a Process, Not an Event

One of CCL's core tenets is that development occurs over time and in stages. While we originally emphasized learning from experience, that's not the only component of leader development. In 1996, our findings were popularized by Robert Eichinger and Michael Lombardo as the framework "70-20-10." They wrote that 70% of developmental learning comes from the experiences of challenging assignments, 20% is the result of developmental relationships (such as a coach, a mentor, or a trusted confidant), and 10% comes from classroom training. But the 70-20-10 ratio isn't based on hard evidence: It's merely shorthand for the situations in which learning can occur. Those different contexts all play a role in development, and we pressed all three into action.

The principle that development wasn't an event but a process fueled our design of the LeaderLab program in 1996, which featured two face-to-face learning group gatherings and the assignment of a "process advisor" to each participant for support between sessions. We detailed the use of process advisors in *Coaching for Action* (1999). Our programs have become known for featuring individualized, one-on-one feedback (assessment) in a safe, supportive setting by a "feedback coach." From that design, two important ideas gained ground: (1) part of a leader's development was to accrue the capacity to coach others; and (2) coaching could be made systemic throughout an organization by institutionalizing it as a development system. We shared those two positions in two books: *The CCL Handbook of Coaching: A Guide for the Leader Coach* (2006) and *The Center for Creative Leadership Handbook of Coaching in Organizations* (2015).

On-the-Job Learning

If development is a process, then what kind of process is it? One answer binds development (the lessons of experience) tightly to the context in which experiences happen. For the most part, that means on the job. Over the years, our LOE research spurred organizations to build and adopt training designs that integrated learning experiences into their leader development programs. Our long relationship with researchers, company HR departments, and other sites of leadership development allowed us to catalog and detail a comprehensive set of models, tools, best practices, and advice that organizations use for on-the-job development. Many are part of *Experience-Driven Leader Development*, published in 2014. Another example of a guide to on-the-job experiences and tactics for making the most of your experiences is *Compass: Your Guide for Leadership Development and Coaching* (2017).

Derailment

While we researched developmental challenges and experiences, we also asked: Were there experiences and behaviors that negatively affect a leader's career? Derailment has been a topic of study in the managerial field since the 1960s, and we were one of the first organizations to systematically study it. It defined leaders who derail when already high on the organizational ladder and who were expected to go even further. The gap between an organization's expectations for a leader's potential and that leader's actual performance is at the core of derailment. We came to understand the factors that cause established or high potential leaders to derail or plateau so that managers could learn to avoid it by meeting their organization's and their own expectations.

An early statement of the derailment research, *Off the Track: Why and How Successful Executives Get Derailed*, appeared in 1983, *The Dynamics of Managerial Derailment* was created in 1988, and *Preventing Derailment* followed in 1996. Our derailment research also included women leaders and different global regions. (Some of that work appeared in *Breaking the Glass Ceiling*, 1987.) In 1996, *A Look at Derailment Today: North America and Europe* was published. Over decades, we applied our derailment research to specific organizational contexts and their impact on derailment, including career stages, managerial levels, generations, and emotional intelligence. We incorporated the findings from those research streams into our Benchmarks assessment and have influenced developmental practices worldwide.

Demonstrating the Impact of Leadership Development

In the mid-1990s, organizations began asking, "Does this leader development stuff work?" CCL had been mindful of this question for some time. From the mid-1980s, we'd conducted in-depth, formal program evaluations to ensure that the solutions we put out to the world were effective. We wanted to fully understand and demonstrate the impact of leadership development activities and become a significant contributor to the "evaluation movement."

We've designed and conducted evaluations in the corporate, government, nonprofit, and educational sectors around the globe, and we've created complex, multifaceted, and longitudinal designs and methods that are culturally and contextually appropriate for intended audiences. Like our leadership development work, our evaluation work expanded from a focus on individual leaders to teams, organizations, and eventually, the societal level. Armed with our knowledge of how learning occurs, we positioned its evaluation practice as continuous improvement and learning. Along the way, we collaborated with colleagues and clients to develop evaluation design, perspective, and tools.

In 1995, we created a 360-degree follow-up instrument called REFLEC-TIONS® to help us measure the behavioral changes of individuals participating in our programs. Our evaluation expertise was made available to the public for practical use in *Evaluating the Impact of Leadership Development: A Professional Guide* (2004). In 2005, we received a grant from The Robert Wood Johnson Foundation to gather leadership development evaluation experts to produce *The Handbook of Leadership Development Evaluation* (2006).

In a series of "framework papers," we leveraged decades of evaluation experience to create architecture to support ideas and practice in the evaluation field. For example, a 2020 paper, "Leadership Development Impact

(LDI) Framework" describes a way for understanding and maximizing the impact of leadership development initiatives at the individual, group, organizational, and societal levels. We further discussed societal impact in a 2022 paper, "Leadership Development as a Lever for Social Change." Longitudinal evaluations of our programs continue, which has led to innovations such as using predictive data analytics to help organizations tailor their leader development strategies. That work is described in a 2018 article, "Using Predictive Analytics."

Our researchers employ novel approaches in their evaluation work, such as using social network analysis to understand how patterns of interaction and collaboration shift over time within organizations. They have applied level-specific evaluations to projects such as the award-winning evaluation of the Bryan Leadership Development Initiative, which provided leadership development for local school leaders, teachers, and administrators in North Carolina. Multiple evaluations of community-based programs like the Bryan Initiative and the Latina Success Leadership Program (see 2023 article), put our approaches into practice, which yields further advances in evaluation methods.

For example, we developed the Community Equity Indicator (CEI) in 2022, which focuses specifically on societal impact and is used to complement other assessments. However, the CEI differs from many other CCL assessments. While most reveal one or more perspectives about individual leaders, the CEI is a collective measurement tool meant to (1) encourage leaders to engage with members of their communities; (2) distribute the required effort of collecting community-focused data across many people; and (3) provide some sense of ownership and connection to the people responding to the survey.

Evaluation research and practice at CCL continues. For example, we follow up with participants two months after a program with a standardized post-program impact survey, Return on Leadership Learning (ROLL). We use the data collected from ROLL to learn more about which programs are least and most effective in helping leaders make positive changes when they return to work. Additionally, we're looking into the critical factors to consider when designing and delivering leadership solutions for neurodivergent leaders.

Creativity and Innovation

CCL's founders were interested in creativity and its relationship to leadership. How can leaders manage the continual reinvention and re-creation required to keep an organization sustainable? During its first decade, we brought inventive minds from around the world to our headquarters in Greensboro, NC, to share their insights. These meetings became annual Creativity Weeks. Gaining firsthand knowledge of the changes organizations face in their daily operations led us to create practical responses to those situations by studying creativity and innovation.

Creativity Week evolved into the Association for Managers of Innovation (AMI) in 1981, and this global community of innovation practitioners still thrives. Connections made through AMI's networking and learning opportunities have created new knowledge about and understanding of the relationship between creativity and leadership.

To share what we learned about creativity from its research into group problem-solving techniques and in collaboration with innovation-minded companies, we designed the Targeted Innovation program (1998-2003) to help teams learn how to adopt the appropriate creative style and technique that fit their situation. Targeted Innovation demonstrated that creativity and innovation are manageable and predictable processes, not random or magical forces. Creativity, like leadership, can be developed.

Similarly, we developed Implementing Innovation in the 1980s to assist product development teams. As part of the program, teams worked through a staged process with a coach and learned about organizational innovation processes and climate. Out of that program, we developed the KEYS® to Creativity and Innovation assessment in 1987 (in collaboration with Dr. Teresa Amabile of the Harvard Business School) to measure the creative climate of an organization — how well it supports creative endeavor and the people engaged in it. The roots of much of our thinking and approach to innovation creative climates can be found in the book *Positive Turbulence* (1999). The book remains a touchstone even as our work in creativity and innovation has evolved along several paths.

CCL launched its Leading Creatively program in 1971 to help leaders learn creative approaches to dealing with change and complexity. During the program's seven-year run, we interviewed the Leading Creatively participants, and our findings resulted in a model of creative leadership described in the 2002 book, *The Leader's Edge*.

Parallel to these developments, CCL had a long-standing "innovation" group connected to its research activities and, at the time of this writing, was part of the Partnerships and Innovation group. But innovation at CCL isn't siloed in a group; we promote innovation across CCL and in all kinds of circumstances, from product development to the design of business processes.

Spanning Boundaries

Mixes of culture, history, ethnicity, and generational perspectives complicate how to lead others. In contemporary organizations, leaders need to create shared direction, alignment, and commitment between groups of people with vastly different lived experiences and values. CCL's early forays into cultural differences resulted in a learning framework published as *Managing Across Cultures* in 1996. Tactics for leading in the changing situation of globalization were published as *Managerial Effectiveness in a Global Context* in 2002.

We launched the Leadership Across Differences (LAD) research in 2001 to expand the understanding and practice of leadership in the context of racial, religious, gender, ethnic, and cultural differences. A diverse team of CCL faculty, working in collaboration with international researchers, collected data from hundreds of employees in for-profit and nonprofit organizations in twelve countries across five continents. The LAD findings highlighted trends of a changing leadership environment that are now accepted as commonplace. It also gave us methods and knowledge for talking explicitly about the difficulties and opportunities that arise when diverse groups meet in the workplace and the kinds of leadership practices and beliefs best suited for navigating and capitalizing on those profound differences. Tactics for applying that knowledge made up *Boundary Spanning Leadership: Six Practices for Solving Problems, Driving Innovation, and Transforming Organizations* (2011). Those tactics were further developed as a practical training tool in the *Boundary Spanning Leadership Workshop Facilitator Kit* in 2017.

Equity, Diversity, and Inclusion in Leadership Ranks

Global telecommunications have made almost every organization multinational. To "lead across difference" is a desired leadership skillset. Relatively early in our history, we created programs for groups traditionally underrepresented in leadership development initiatives. *Breaking the Glass Ceiling* was published in 1987. Research into women leaders led to a leadership development program fashioned around their specific challenges. The Executive Women's Workshop (1988) was later developed into the Women's Leadership Program (retired in 2015) and developed further into the Women's Leadership Experience (2015-2020). Our African American Leadership Program ran from 1995-2008. In that program, participants learned (among other things) how race influences their leadership style and how others may perceive their skills as a leader.

The release of *Standing at the Crossroads* (2002) and *Leading in Black and White* (2003) bolstered our single-identity programs. The research on women leaders generated further insights into the value of holding multiple roles outside one's job for improving leadership effectiveness (e.g., parent or community volunteer). Those findings contributed to work-life integration research and new ideas imagined as "holistic" leadership development.

As part of its diversifying research, and notable among its research efforts in Asia, our BOLD 3.0: Future Fluent Board Leadership in Asia study examined challenges faced by corporate boards in Asia. Researchers interviewed and surveyed more than 400 organizations. The project's key findings were that boards lack leadership, oversight, and diversity due to cultural pressures and ownership structures. Those results suggested changes to prepare boards to focus more on future readiness. In 2019, we published a report on the work called "*Bold 3.0: Future-fluent Board Leadership in Asia.*"

More recent research has looked at the idea of "organizational citizen behavior," or OCB. This concept describes employees who go beyond formal job requirements — pitching in to help colleagues, volunteering for extra tasks, etc. We examined negative aspects of OCB, such as its tendency to place women in the role of supporting men. While women's slower career advancement is often explained by bias, career choices, greater caretaking responsibilities, and work-family decisions, our research into OCB suggests other reasons. Women who are "good organizational citizens" typically do not receive recognition or career advancement for their help and face backlash when they don't help.

Differences among people can often be a plus in an organization because such differences bring a mix of new ideas and proven tactics that spark innovation. But the social implications surrounding diversity don't stop at any organization's front door. In the mid-1990s, our researchers examined the effect of diversity on work team productivity, including psychological diversity. They also examined the experiences of expatriates, the demands of leading global teams and workforces, and cultural adaptability. Findings from these different research streams were captured in a book sponsored by a grant from the American Psychological Association (*Diversity in Work Teams: Research Paradigms for a Changing Workplace*, 1995) and in the release of *Success for the New Global Manager* (2002).

More recently, we developed the REAL™ framework in 2023 to help leaders and their organizations move beyond abstract egalitarian ideals. The REAL acronym represents four areas of EDI (equity, diversity, and inclusion) focus: **R**eveal relevant opportunities; **E**levate equity; **A**ctivate diversity; and **L**ead inclusively. It's designed to help make EDI culture change real to the people in the organization. (CCL uses the EDI acronym, rather than the more common DEI, to emphasize equity.) Our research shows that a feeling of belonging has a positive effect on an organization's culture and helps retain committed, energized, resilient employees. A 2023 article, "The Research Foundations for REAL," describes the framework and how it can be used to make EDI efforts tangible and practical.

Generations at Work

The leadership development needs, values, and learning styles of the different generations interacting in the workplace are examples of another kind of diversity. Our researchers asked whether the attitudes toward, among, and between generations were mired in assumptions, anecdotes, and misunderstanding, not in critical differences. We've approached organizations in

64 countries to participate in surveys about learning styles and leadership across generations.

Insight gleaned from our generational research helped us design best-practice leadership development initiatives for up-and-coming managers, as well as inform organizations through such publications as *Retiring the Generation Gap: How Employees Young and Old Can Find Common Ground* (2007) and *What Millennials Want from Work: How to Maximize Engagement in Today's Workforce* (2017). We've conducted more than 10,000 surveys and scores of in-depth interviews to grasp the perspectives, goals, and developmental and leadership challenges for leaders early in their careers.

Some of our related work includes participating in the 2021 Asia-Europe Meeting and partnering with other like-minded organizations to release the 2021 *ASEM Youth Report: For Young People, By Young People*. The report captures the leadership experiences, aspirations, and recommendations for a post-COVID-19 world from young people, which organizations can be mindful of as they move into the future.

Connected Leadership

The connections and similarities among several streams of CCL work — teams, groups, organizational systems, and complex challenges — suggested that integrating those streams might spawn new understanding and practice. In 2002, under the umbrella of Connected Leadership, we reached three important outcomes: a new leadership framework, a new concept of leadership culture, and new practices to facilitate organizational change.

In 2008, concepts emerging from Connected Leadership and our own research into "relational leadership" led us to create a practical framework for putting those ideas into action: Direction – Alignment – Commitment (DAC)™. The theory supporting DAC appeared in a widely read and influential 2008 article in *The Leadership Quarterly*, "Developing the theory and practice of leadership development: A relational view." A practical guide to the DAC ideas, *Direction, Alignment, Commitment: Achieving Better Results through Leadership* was first published in 2015 and revised in 2020.

Our Leadership Culture Model also emerged from the Connected

Leadership project and describes how leadership cultures can transform to deal more effectively with complex strategic issues. Each stage represents a revised set of beliefs and practices for how DAC is produced. In this progression, the cultural view of "what is leadership" begins with command and control (dependent), which is superseded by one of mutual influence (independent), which in turn progresses to a view of leadership as a fundamentally collective activity (interdependent). The framework is particularly useful for helping groups examine their assumptions about leadership and for highlighting that leadership development involves not only the development of individuals but also the development of leadership cultures.

These two frameworks — and tools developed from them — supported a robust organizational leadership development practice to augment our existing individual leader development practice. Core to this practice was our leadership strategy work with executive teams struggling to implement strategies in uncertain and volatile circumstances and organizational transformation work to engage executives in a deep look at their own need to change. This work helps organizations build a coalition of committed leaders to communicate, guide, and implement organizational change.

Team research, inter-organizational social networks and network analysis, sensemaking, and dialogue all came into focus under the Connected Leadership banner. Essential to that view was how leadership operates through (and is visible in) networks of personal, professional, and reporting relationships in organizations. Relationships operate in organizations as a means of getting work done, but they don't always show up in an organizational chart. We've studied topics like gender differences in networks, how boundary spanning networks drive organizational change and effectiveness, advanced network analytics and data science, and the social networks of top executives. By integrating these research streams under the connected leadership label, we intended to help organizations achieve greater collaboration and engagement across boundaries and improve dialogue and learning, while embracing differences and creating the means for involving people at all levels of the organization in leadership work.

In 2014, CCL and the University of Cincinnati hosted a Thought Forum on Network Leadership and Leadership Networks. Scholars from around the globe brought diverse perspectives and knowledge from a variety of contexts and settings, including corporate, government, military, intelligence, large and small community-based organizations, and social movements. Themes and future directions that emerged during the forum informed a *Leadership Quarterly* special issue on collective and network approaches to leadership in 2016.

Team Effectiveness

Perhaps nowhere is the relational nature of leadership more visible than on a team. Aside from the usual factors that support high-performing teams (established norms, defined expectations, and accountability), consider the social dynamics of people working together to achieve a common goal. Our ideas of DAC speak to team relationships, as direction, alignment, and commitment are hallmarks of a successful team.

Leadership is the domain of teams, not single leaders. Successful projects often rely on a network of teams that cross functions, time zones, and organizational boundaries. High-performing organizations emphasize collaboration within and across teams, enabling the output of the whole to be greater than the sum of its parts. In a 2022 CCL survey, 89% of managers said cross-team collaboration was important, and our research indicates that most obstacles to good teamwork are the result of poor collaboration inside the team. Sometimes, poor collaboration derives from a lack of trust among members. But while 80% of the managers we surveyed said it took time to develop trust, we found ample evidence that trust could be built rather quickly.

In 2019, we developed Team Vantage, which we added to our Leadership at the Peak (LAP) program (1985). This assessment diagnoses senior team strengths, climates, and connections from multiple perspectives. Through ongoing research, Team Vantage has evolved into a powerful diagnostic tool for senior teams seeking to improve the team's connections.

Our research into teams has shifted with trends in organizational structures, such as the virtual teams common to global teams and hybrid work teams, which rose in the post-pandemic period as the number of remote workers increased dramatically. The Virtual Teams Polarity project learned from 141 virtual teams across the globe, from multiple industries and sectors, to build the foundation for online programs that help teams adjust to working virtually.

Studying polarities illustrated the paradoxes especially potent in times of crisis or uncertainty. Findings showed that duality thinking — a yes/no dichotomy — is more limiting than a view that accounts for how each side of a situation influences the other. Teams are constantly negotiating the push and pull of this dynamic polarity, but understanding and using polarities can help teams manage unsolvable tensions and improve performance over time. Examples of this work are described in "How to Lead Virtual Teams: The Power of Leveraging Polarities and Individual Paradoxes" (2018), as well as in "Pandemic Paradoxes and How They Affect Your Workers" and "Leading in A Crisis: From Survival to Strategic Pivot" (focusing specifically on Asian leaders), both published in 2020. Whatever the environment, we continually examine practices and beliefs about team formation, commitment, norms, conflict, psychological safety, and team motivational development — all crucial to team performance.

Our practical insights into teams express four important parts of team leadership that produce results because they drive collective achievement:

- **Collective Mindset:** Team members' beliefs about how they work together.

- **Connection:** How the team's work integrates with the organization and beyond.

- **Core:** Why the team was formed.

- **Cohesion:** The approach team members take when working together.

Organizations with the most skilled, agile, and networked teams can meet the challenges of collaboration and group direction with capability, speed, and efficiency. Whatever the environment, CCL research lays out the kinds of teams and team leadership that can produce successful results.

Leadership Resilience and Well-being

We've used the phrase "holistic leadership" to refer to the full human measure of leadership readiness and performance. Along with on-the-job development, holistic leadership includes lessons of experience gained outside of work and how leaders can use them to develop at-work behaviors and perspectives. It also includes the leader's inner world: the effects of hardships and the recovery from them and the effects of health on leadership performance. (An introduction to this area of research appeared in a 2014 CCL article, "Leadership Development Beyond Competencies.")

Early in the LOE research project, a category of "personal experiences" emerged as a cluster of experiences leaders agree are developmental — an especially relevant finding for women leaders. Their general cultural history of child rearing and home management was often disregarded in appraising their managerial talents. The practical benefits of nonwork experiences appear in *Learning from Life* (2000).

Our research has also probed hidden skillsets and hardwired behaviors that leaders can learn to manage to meet the complicated challenges they often face. We've investigated such topics as sleep habits, mindfulness, the operation of the parasympathetic nervous system, the field of neuroscience, work-life balance, personal health, and more.

Cognitive Distortions and Regulating Emotions

When performing at their best, leaders avoid common thinking traps (cognitive distortions) in order to act and communicate clearly when facing dilemmas and strategic challenges. Cognitive distortions, such as all-or-nothing thinking, blaming others, or jumping to conclusions, interfere with the clear-eyed thinking leaders often depend on.

Our research indicates cognitive distortions affect how leaders view their role, see conflict, perceive organizational support, and measure job satisfaction and can lead to burnout. Leaders who practice reframing tactics and create distance from emotional reactions to view situations objectively can regulate their emotional responses. That's not the same as suppressing emotional responses, which research says isn't effective. We published our findings in a 2020 report called "The Stories We Tell."

Stress and Burnout

Over the years, our work has addressed stress and burnout in myriad ways. A short article on the subject, "Stress and the Eye of the Beholder," was published in 1987 and suggested *how* leaders see a situation affects the level of stress they feel. Following that article, we analyzed the consequences of burnout — specifically the relation of emotional exhaustion, depersonalization, and reduced accomplishment to job satisfaction. To create a full picture, we also examined the antecedents of burnout and its stages.

In some cases, we examined the impact stress has on the health of a leader and how to mitigate those effects. A practical guide, *Managing Leadership Stress,* was published in 2008. In 2016, we shared some of its insight into the effects of stress on brain health in "The Care and Feeding of the Leader's Brain." Between 2008 and 2012, CCL researchers worked with Ellen Kossek of Purdue University on issues of work-life balance, often a cause of stress. That work led to the Work-Life Indicator (WLI) in 2011. That tool can be used to frame discussions of work-life issues and the setting of work-life goals. *Managing Your Whole Life* (2013) is a brief guide to the ideas behind WLI.

Grief

We've long known about the potential of hardships to generate lessons. In the shadow of the COVID-19 pandemic, we investigated grief as a specific hardship. The COVID-19 pandemic meant many employees carried their grief to work. What can a leader do for their workers that goes beyond policy? How can leaders develop and apply empathy to help a grieving worker manage their healing while still being effective? How can a leader offer full support to a grieving person and manage the tasks of the organization? In a 2023 *Journal of Management Inquiry* article, "Monday mourning," our researchers encouraged more studies into bereavement in the workplace. They suggested several paths toward better understanding how to address the needs of bereaved employees with organizational policies and practices.

We've also examined grief as an aspect of transformation and learning — a grief quite different from personal loss. During times of change, people must let go of old ways and embrace new ones. Transitional experiences of grief don't rise to the level of personal loss, but they are challenging. Leaders must step outside of their comfort zones and embrace the messy mistakes of learning through experience. These examples make up some of the discussion in our book *Leading with Authenticity in Times of Transition* (2005).

Resilience

Resilience has held interest among CCL researchers for a long time and is implied in the hardship-to-learning path we blazed with LOE. What lesson can be learned from hardship if you can't pick yourself up from that experience? Building resilience in today's increasingly uncertain and complex world is crucial, especially for those in leadership positions.

Our research found evidence supporting eight practices to help leaders build resilience: sleep, physical activity, mindfulness, cognitive reappraisal, savoring, gratitude, social connection, and social contact. The research behind the eight practices is detailed in the 2021 book *Resilience that Works: Eight Practices for Leadership and Life*.

Leadership in the Digital Age

Since our earliest days, CCL has integrated technological advancements into our research and our assessments, and continued to explore how new technologies might enhance leadership development. For example, we launched the World Leadership Survey (WLS), an online globally available survey, to collect data on leadership practices, behaviors, and attitudes across cultures. The data leaders provided through WLS between 2010-2014 shed light on workplace attitudes, workforce and employee engagement, retention, trust, corporate social responsibility, implicit leadership theories, opinions on what makes an effective leader, and more.

Our research on the role of employee motivation and engagement and their effect on work attitudes and performance extended past the WLS. Studies reveal the complexity of work motivation and engagement processes, which are influenced by both individual differences and organizational situations. Motivation and engagement are multifaceted; individual dispositions and organizational contexts shape employees' motivation, which impacts workplace attitudes and performance.

We've also added personal technologies to our research toolkit. These additions accompany the technology we already had integrated with our work, including assessment data results and analysis, distance learning, and other refinements. Self-tracking wearables, for example, quantify people's everyday experiences and behaviors and offer feedback for improvement. Insights people gain from the data wearables generate help them exercise more regularly, improve their sleep habits, check overall health, and improve aspects of their mental health. Given all the tools for self-reporting feedback, we asked: Why not use these tools for leadership development?

To answer that question, we looked at how pairing technologies to real-time, on-the-job assessments, such as feedback, could help leaders develop continuously. We sharpened our view of development on the job as it investigated how leaders might learn from their own data without relying on experts, coaches, or bosses. An introduction to our use of these technologies is expressed in a 2019 CCL article, "The Quantified Leader: Wearables & Self-Tracking Technology for Development."

The advent of sensor-enabled technology furthered our research and practice in areas such as resilience and emotional intelligence. In one instance, we used AI to review and synthesize patterns in a leader's speech, writing, and presentations. Our researchers assessed theoretical insights into technology-enhanced leadership development and published their findings in a 2021 journal article, "Sounds like a Leader." We also reported on what our research says about applying technologies for development purposes in "Leadership Development in the Flow of Work: Leveraging Technology to Accelerate Learning" (2022) and "Six Strategies for Digital Learning Success" (2019).

The behavioral changes we specialize in are often best achieved through face-to-face encounters, but the availability of technology-based tools that support distance learning and virtual face-to-face encounters continues to multiply and grow more sophisticated. We recognized the importance of communications technology to the field of leadership development long before the technological advances we now take for granted.

We've been working to integrate technological advances into distance learning or coaching for several years — not to find a place in the technology parade, but to address the question of how to improve the tools of leadership development. Distance learning and "blended learning" (combining virtual with face-to-face interactions) present challenges and opportunities. In 2001, we received an Excellence in Practice Award from the American Society for Training and Development for the blended learning design of the Xerox Emerging Leaders Program, which ran from 1999 to 2008. We've developed webinars and web-based goal management systems to extend the development process beyond classroom events.

Integrating technology with our research into leadership development set the stage for our CCL Leadership Accelerator (CLA). As a digital learning platform, CLA leans on the essential on-the-job development approach proven in our research and practice. Lessons in CLA connect with leadership challenges that learners identify as important to their development and performance, and because developmental relationships play a critical role in learning to lead, CLA supports discussion threads featuring incentives that keep learners engaged. With CLA, as with many of its digital products and research initiatives, it becomes much easier to track learner data, which we use to constantly improve our research and product designs.

As mentioned earlier, we've used machine learning and predictive analytics to help organizations better understand and create the leadership development needed for their future. Our researchers asked several questions, including: How should managers and executives lead to grow their organization's competitive advantage? How can an organization shape its leadership culture to drive sustained, profitable growth in years to come? What practices will retain and engage top talent?

In pursuing answers, we used predictive analytics to help organizations connect people data with actual business results. By making those connections visible, organizations would be able to better use the strengths of their leaders, and management could more strategically decide which HR investments are most likely to move the organization where it wants and needs to go. The results were specific leadership development plans that helped organizations reap a return on their investment in leadership development.

Leadership Challenges

Textbook notions of how managers learn and how they might advance their careers were challenged as global changes once on the horizon in the 1970s and 80s — demographic shifts, international expansions, and technology — became commonplace. Changes like these show no sign of slowing.

We've long recognized leadership appears and works differently among multiple contexts. In response, our research agenda reflects an international perspective on key leadership and leadership development issues worldwide — some of the toughest challenges of the 21st century. We've looked deeply into these issues across diverse political, economic, and social boundaries to understand the connections between individual, organizational, and societal transformation. Our goal has been to enrich the understanding of what it means to lead in today's complex, international, multicultural environment and to share those insights as broadly as possible.

While globalization in the 1980s and after made cross-cultural and multinational leadership relevant, the unforeseen global challenge of the COVID-19 pandemic of 2019-2022 made cross-cultural and multinational leadership critical. COVID drastically changed leadership structures by endorsing the widespread use of remote workforces that lack the usual organizational ties to missions and values (platforms such as Uber also played a role in expanding a "gig economy"). Whether these changes are long-lived is still to be seen, but there's no question about their profound impact. Our research and practice keep pace by renewing and expanding our keen observations of the contemporary workplace.

For example, one result of our research into Asian organizations shows how leadership can be effective in a hybrid workforce. A report on that work, *Work 3.0: Reimagining Leadership in a Hybrid World*, was published in 2022.

Our presence in Asia was a response to that region's growing influence. We were awarded a substantial Research Incentive Scheme for Companies (RISC) grant from the Singapore Economic Development Board in 2003, which enabled us to set up our Singapore office that year and begin pivotal Asia-focused research projects: Understanding the Leadership Gap, Lessons of Experience-Asia, and Bridging Cultural Boundaries. By 2007, we brought our LDP program to Singapore. The Asia-based research led to the development of the Leadership Gap Indicator™ assessment in 2009.

Our 2010 book *Developing Tomorrow's Leaders Today* detailed critical lessons drawn from the experiences of senior Indian business leaders. We partnered with the Tata Management Training Center in Pune, India to implement the LOE research from that book. Tools such as *Experience Explorer* (2014) also drew from that research and made it applicable to audiences beyond Asia.

We hosted the 2011 International Academy of Intercultural Research conference in Singapore and brought the LAP program to Singapore in 2012. That same year, we launched the Global Citizen Leader program at Welingkar Institute of Management Development (WeSchool) in Mumbai and at the Institute for Future Education Entrepreneurship and Leadership (iFEEL) in Lonavala, India.

We opened an office in China in 2013, started work in Sri Lanka in 2014, and began the Global Asian Leader research project in 2018. Based on interviews about the challenges and barriers to leadership in Asia, the research supplies a framework to develop the required global leadership capabilities. It's described in a research report from that year, *The Global Asian Leader: From Local Star to Global CXO*. In 2022, we launched its Global Asian Leader program for the Asia Pacific region, which we reported on in *The Global Asian Leader 2.0: From Asia, for the World*.

Top Leaders Face Unique Challenges

Senior leaders must be able to see changes and challenges coming and ensure their staff can prepare, respond, and adapt. For some time, we've believed there's a qualitative difference in the experience of being "at the top" as opposed to "near the top," particularly in terms of development. The higher one goes up the ladder, for example, the harder it is to receive accurate developmental feedback. In response, we studied the experiences of high-level executives to develop knowledge and services to address their development needs. We detailed this research in a report, *High Hurdles: The Challenge of Executive Self-Development* (1985), which formed the basis of the book *Beyond Ambition: How Driven Managers Can Lead Better and Live Better* (1991).

The method used in *High Hurdles* included interviewing co-workers and family members of participating executives as well as the executives themselves. The goal was to learn about the leader from multiple perspectives and in multiple settings. As happened with LGI, research participants expressed interest in what was learned about them and wanted to use that information to develop themselves.

This research produced the Awareness Program for Executive Excellence (APEX)®, which made its appearance in 1985 as a special engagement with one of our clients. APEX was highly individualized as a program, and each senior executive who took part in APEX received the perspectives of two CCL coaches who led them through the process of analyzing their feedback and strategizing how to put what they learned into practice.

The LAP program became a laboratory for studying specialized topics such as executive selection, fitness for leadership, and executive tenure. We developed Benchmarks® for Executives™ when we found that the development needs of very top-level participants were distinctive from other executive levels.

Over approximately ten years, we collaborated with top-level leaders to develop new knowledge about complexity and organizational practices. That led to a study of strategic leadership, an advanced skill in top leadership. We pushed our strategic leadership ideas beyond senior leadership ranks when we observed that strategic leadership responsibilities were increasingly being pushed down into lower levels of organizations. We used that insight to design the Developing the Strategic Leader program (2002-2013), which served all levels of leaders.

We discussed our findings on strategy and leadership in *Becoming a Strategic Leader: Your Role in Your Organization's Enduring Success* (2005; 2014). The book describes strategy as a learning process that combines specific levels of thinking, acting, and influencing — all of which can be developed in leaders throughout their organizations.

First-Time Managers Have Their Own Challenges

First-time managers have special challenges of their own. We saw leaders who didn't occupy senior ranks as an expansion of the population eligible for leadership development. Top-level and first-time leaders hold one thing in common: it's difficult to get developmental feedback. Top leaders can become isolated from honest appraisal of their performance, and most new leaders haven't set up the feedback network they need to continue their development (and their company hasn't, either).

In 2010, we introduced the program Maximizing Your Leadership Potential (MLP) to fill that developmental gap. New leaders attending the program (in person or virtually) learn how personal strengths and weaknesses affect their team leadership. They practice essential leadership skills, such as communication, and they learn to give feedback that affects the people they manage. MLP incorporates 360-degree feedback and stresses collaboration, influence skills, and conflict management.

The data we collected during the MLP program laid the ground for the 2016 book *Be the Boss Everyone Wants to Work For*. We continued this cycle of ideas into action by creating CCL Boost™ in 2017, an online leadership course for new leaders. First-time managers attend the program because the skills, knowledge, and perspectives that helped them land their new leadership role aren't necessarily the same ones that will help them perform at their best or advance in their careers.

The Ladder of Challenge and Learning

Our work to name developmental experiences, beginning with LOE, continues. For our Leadership Challenge Ladder project, we used AI to rapidly sweep data collected from over 37,000 multi-level leaders working in more than 6,000 organizations from 2010-2021 (details of the work appeared in the 2021 "Leadership Challenge Ladder (LCL) Technical Report."). The Leadership Challenge Ladder framework (2023) was derived from leaders' responses to the question, "What are the three most critical leadership challenges you are currently facing?" We pinpointed 42 challenges that persist over time and across different industries and sectors. The lessons leaders glean from those challenges serve an important developmental purpose. While more research is needed, this project suggests that organizations can take a targeted approach toward designing efficient and cost-effective development strategies.

Leaders and Organizational Change

Our approach to addressing change has been twofold: one, to help leaders manage their own responses to change and to recognize responses in the people they lead to help the entire team transition to new circumstances; and two, to examine organizational environments, cultures, and climates to help organizations develop leadership talent for managing change. During times of change, leaders must deal with reactions — such as fear, frustration, resentment, distrust, and a sense of unfairness and betrayal — and organizational processes are inadequate to meet these challenges. Faced with the turmoil of change, leaders must focus on the emotional aspects of change: grieving, letting go, building hope, and learning. Our guidance for how to think about and how to address the emotional fallout of change was published in *Leading with Authenticity in Times of Transition* (2005). Individual leaders can also learn to deal with multiple changes simultaneously (the usual way of change) with the counsel of the 2015 book, *Leading Continuous Change*.

On the systems side, most change efforts fail because they use methods better suited to single challenges that occur in a linear way; but change is a constant stream of challenges. Change exerts pressure on strategy, tactics, and even culture. *Transforming Your Leadership Culture* (2009) described our work with organizations that were implementing change efforts at a complex, systemic level. Evidence indicates that to transform an organization, its culture must change; and for culture to change, the top leaders responsible for leading the effort must change themselves.

Organizational transformation (and individual change, for that matter) is complicated and, at times, complex. As our work has evolved over the decades, we've clarified the links between leadership, creativity, change, and complexity. The Navigating Complex Challenges program (2006-2008), for example, gave leaders the opportunity to focus on their organizations' real-life leadership dilemmas arising from the complicated situations their organizations continually faced. Change faces leaders at all levels, wrapped in the complexities of technology, diversity, and competition. To make the changes needed to thrive, personally and organizationally, leaders must create the change they want to see in the organization. We agree with others who say, "Change happens from the inside → out."

The Boldness
of Uncertain
Potentialities

S ince its founding, CCL has entertained unproven but promising ideas
and asked questions without simple answers. Today, our research
agenda continues CCL's 50-year legacy in leadership development
worldwide. The purpose is still the same as it was at the start in the early
1970s: to generate powerful insights and practical wisdom that help people,
organizations, and communities address their challenges, perform better,
and adapt to changing conditions.

Our research keeps us grounded in the practical application of our
work: turning ideas into action. It prioritizes four interrelated areas: (1)
research and analysis using such methods as experiments, surveys, interviews, and data science to build frameworks for theory and practice; (2)
evaluating a program's impact on managers, leaders, and their organizations
through surveys, interviews, focus groups, and data analytics; (3) provid-
ing subject matter expertise to clients and faculty by creating workshop
and classroom modules, designing programs for the public and customizing
them for individual organizations, and developing tools and assessments for
the practical application of knowledge; and (4) sharing research insights in
the form of papers, posts on CCL's research blog and on CCL.org, articles in

the popular press and in academic journals, conference presentations, webinars, and books.

Our researchers continue to open new lines of inquiry into areas of particular importance to the development and practice of leadership and relevant to the times we live in. What will come from the answers is uncertain, but we see tremendous potential for making positive changes and furthering our mission. What follows is a brief on the areas of inquiry we will take on in the years ahead.

Leading for an Equitable Future

Understanding the interplay of social identities, interpersonal experiences, organizational practices, and societal factors can make greater impact possible for organizations and create a higher purpose for the people who work in them. But when are organizational EDI efforts cosmetic (supplying evidence of compliance to EDI efforts), when do they open conversation (sharing stories and experiences to create psychological safety from which people can learn), and when do they signal commitment (indicated by concrete action that sustains EDI efforts)? In seeking answers, CCL has named organizational "fault lines," tracked and measured organizations' EDI outcomes, and provided concrete steps for organizational change.

Our longstanding research across cultures, genders, generations, and other differences positions us to find answers to such questions as:

- What enables and hinders sustained equity, diversity, and inclusion in organizations?

- How are organizations evolving their EDI metrics in response to social movements?

- How can we measure helping behaviors equitably for employees of all genders?

- Can efforts to help students see the usefulness and relevance of what they're learning mitigate socioeconomic disparities? Can such efforts increase students' motivation and engagement by connecting the material to their personal values, goals, and interests?

- How can data help ensure leadership assessments are valid and fair across diverse populations?

- How can leaders mitigate bias when applying AI to strategic decisions?

Maximizing Leadership Development Impact

We continue to research what types of development initiatives work best under what conditions. By understanding the gap between outcomes and expectations and the role of developmental experiences in bridging that gap, organizations, leaders, and the field of leadership development can make more productive decisions about how to approach, practice, and evaluate their work. In the future, we will investigate such questions as:

- How can positive and negative leadership development experiences inform greater effectiveness?

- How can we accurately and longitudinally measure and show leadership growth?

- What does the evidence reveal about coaching's stand-alone effectiveness for leadership development?

- Can episodic memory improve 360-degree feedback?

- How can AI tools augment leadership development?

- How can leadership development employ AI ethically and center it on human interests?

Leading Through Change and into the Future

Throughout our history, we've researched how to equip leaders to navigate change and evolve their organizations amid ever-shifting contexts. For example, before the global COVID-19 pandemic, leading remote workforces received little attention despite rising globalization and digitalization. Now, that change is upon us, with little warning.

Our researchers are exploring the skills, behaviors, and perspectives leaders need to guide transformations. Our earlier work generated insights into change and its consequences at individual, organizational, and societal levels. With cascading crises and disruptive technologies like AI, leaders need the foresight that readies them to build adaptive, human-centered, ethical cultures. How can organizations promote an integrated and comprehensive understanding of leadership capable of navigating complex challenges? Answers to these questions can help:

- How do we develop and prepare leaders and organizations to successfully and sustainably navigate the cascading crises we face today and those to come?

- What is grief's impact on employees, and how can organizations supply meaningful bereavement support?

- Which future leadership skills and perspectives will be most critical to organizational and social sustainability?

- Which trends should leaders focus on to prepare for the future?

- What motivates and deters leaders from adopting AI?

- How are leaders using AI capabilities to manage large-scale change?

- What recent AI advances should inform leadership, and how are researchers applying AI methods today?

- What novel challenges will leaders face in the AI era of tomorrow?

Leading Together

We continue to examine the elements that foster the development of individual people into high-performing teams. We're also researching group capabilities that support distributed leadership responsibilities among teams or group members. More than 96% of working adults collaborate in groups or teams. Leaders and organizations must be able to assess, foster, and use the power of collective leadership to achieve their goals. Our continuing work with teams — in-person, virtual, or hybrids of the two — positions us to better pursue ideas about the social process at the heart of leadership. We seek insight into questions such as:

- How do team behaviors in group settings relate to overall team effectiveness?

- How do team members balance taskwork and team development?

- Can AI and data science illuminate team dynamics and effectiveness?

- When can AI improve coordination and knowledge sharing on distributed teams?

Still a Beginning

CL began as an idea with unproven promise and has grown to a global institution. To meet whatever needs leaders and organizations of the future may have, we build cross-cultural research teams that are generationally, historically, and ethnically diverse.

As the first quarter of the 21st century draws to a close, leaders find themselves operating in an ever-changing world, and we believe effective leadership should change with it. Technological change has accelerated the adoption of remote work, leaders are struggling with the demands of constant communication, and we're all seeking to understand the potential and pitfalls of the yet not fully defined advent of artificial intelligence. CCL's work presents and continues to reveal with greater precision a well-studied collection of behaviors and beliefs that create leadership among people working together. Despite technological and cultural changes, leadership is still people working with other people, and leadership never stops. We all have a stake in ensuring the continued benefits of leadership to achieve prosperity, health, community, and peace — a ripple effect of positive change that matters for all.

Chronological List of Sources

1971. Center for Creative Leadership. *Leading Creatively*. Center for Creative Leadership.

1974. Center for Creative Leadership. *Leadership Development Program*. Center for Creative Leadership.

1978. Morrison, A. M., McCall, M. W., & DeVries, D. L. *Feedback to Managers: A Comprehensive Review of Twenty-four Instruments*. Center for Creative Leadership.

1979. Center for Creative Leadership. *Looking Glass, Inc.* Center for Creative Leadership.

1983. McCall Jr., M. W., & Lombardo, M. M. *Off the Track: Why and How Successful Executives Get Derailed*. Center for Creative Leadership.

1985. Center for Creative Leadership. *Leadership at the Peak*. Center for Creative Leadership.

1985. Kaplan, R. E., Drath, W. H., & Kofodimos, J. R. *High Hurdles: The Challenge of Executive Self-development*. Center for Creative Leadership.

1986. Center for Creative Leadership. *Skillscope Technical Manual*. Center for Creative Leadership.

1987. Amabile, T. *KEYS to Creativity and Innovation Facilitators Guide*. Center for Creative Leadership.

1987.   Lindsey, E. H., Homes, V., & McCall, M. W. *Key Events in Executives' Lives*. Center for Creative Leadership.

1987.   McCauley, C. D. *Stress and the Eye of the Beholder*. Center for Creative Leadership.

1987.   Morrison, A. M., White, R. P., & Van Velsor, E. *Breaking the Glass Ceiling: Can Women Reach the Top of America's Largest Corporations?* Addison-Wesley.

1988.   Lombardo, M. M., & McCauley, C. D. *The Dynamics of Management Derailment*. Center for Creative Leadership.

1988.   Lombardo, M.M., Usher, C., & McCauley, C.D. *Benchmarks Technical Manual*. Center for Creative Leadership.

1989.   Lombardo, M. M., & Eichinger, R. W. *Preventing Derailment: What to Do Before It's Too Late*. Center for Creative Leadership.

1989.   McCauley, C. D., Lombardo, M. M., & Usher, C. J. Diagnosing Management Development Needs: An Instrument Based on How Managers Develop. *Journal of Management*, 15(3), 389-403.

1991.   Kaplan, B., Drath, W., & Kofodimos, J. R. *Beyond Ambition: How Driven Managers Can Lead Better and Live Better* Jossey-Bass.

1991.   Van Velsor, E., & Leslie, J. B., *Feedback to Managers* (2nd ed). Vol. 1, *A guide to Evaluating Multi-rater Feedback Instruments*, and Vol. 2, *A Review and Comparison of Sixteen Multi-rater Feedback Instruments*. Center for Creative Leadership.

1992.   Bunker, K. A., & Webb, A. D. *Learning How to Learn from Experience: Impact of Stress and Coping*. Center for Creative Leadership.

1992.   Dalton, M. *Learning Tactics Inventory Facilitators Guide*. Center for Creative Leadership.

1992.   Morrison, A. M. *The New Leaders: Guidelines on Leadership Diversity in America*. Jossey-Bass.

1993.   Tornow, W. W. (Ed.). Special Issue on 360-degree Feedback. *Human Resource Management*, 32, 2-3.

1994.   Drath, W. H., & Palus, C. J. *Making Common Sense: Leadership as Meaning-Making in a Community of Practice*. Center for Creative Leadership.

1995. Center for Creative Leadership. *Reflections.* Center for Creative Leadership.

1995. Jackson, S. E., & Ruderman, M. N. (Eds.). *Diversity in Work Teams: Research Paradigms for a Changing Workplace.* American Psychological Association.

1995. McCall, M.W., Spreitzer, G.M., & Mahoney. *Prospector.* Center for Creative Leadership.

1996. Leslie, J. B., & Van Velsor, E. *A Look at Derailment Today: North America and Europe.* Center for Creative Leadership.

1996. Lombardo, M.M., & Eichinger, R.W. *Career Architect Development Planner.* Korn Ferry.

1996. Morrison, A. M. *The New Leaders: Leadership Diversity in America.* Jossey-Bass.

1996. Wilson, M. S., Hoppe, M. H., & Sayles, L. R. *Managing Across Cultures: A Learning Framework.* Center for Creative Leadership.

1998. Leslie, J. B., & Fleenor, J. W. *Feedback to Managers: A Review and Comparison of Multi-rater Instruments for Management Development* (3rd ed). Center for Creative Leadership.

1998. McCauley, C. D., Moxley, R. S., Van Velsor, E. (Eds.). *The Center for Creative Leadership Handbook of Leadership Development* (1st ed). Jossey-Bass.

1998. Tornow, W.W. & London, M. (Eds.). *Maximizing the Value of 360-degree Feedback: A Process for Successful Individual and Organizational Development.* Jossey-Bass.

1999. Gryskiewicz, S. S. *Positive Turbulence: Developing Climates for Creativity, Innovation, and Renewal.* Jossey-Bass.

1999. Guthrie, V. A. *Coaching for action: A Report on Long-term Advising in a Program Context.* Center for Creative Leadership.

2000. Center for Creative Leadership. *Executive Dimensions Technical Manual.* Center for Creative Leadership.

2000. Ruderman, M., & Ohlott, P. *Learning From Life: Turning Life's Lessons Into Leadership Experience.* Center for Creative Leadership.

2001. Campbell D. Foreword. In D. Bracken, C. Timmreck & A. Church (Eds.), *The Handbook of Multisource Feedback.* Jossey-Bass.

2001. Center for Creative Leadership. *360 By Design Technical Manual.* Center for Creative Leadership.

2001. Center for Creative Leadership. *360 By Design Technical Manual.* Center for Creative Leadership.

2002. Dalton, M. A., & Center for Creative Leadership (Eds.). *Success for the new Global Manager: What You Need to Know to Work Across Distances, Countries, and Cultures.* Jossey-Bass.

2002. Leslie, J. B., Dalton, M., Ernst, C., & Deal, J. *Managerial Effectiveness in a Global Context.* Center for Creative Leadership.

2002. Palus, C. J., & Horth, D. M. *The Leader's Edge: Six Creative Competencies for Navigating Complex Challenges.* Jossey-Bass.

2002. Ruderman, M. N., & Ohlott, P. J. *Standing at the Crossroads: Next Steps for High-Achieving Women.* Jossey-Bass.

2003. Livers, A. B., & Caver, K. A. *Leading in Black and White: Working Across the Racial Divide in Corporate America.* Jossey-Bass.

2004. Martineau, J., & Hannum, K. *Evaluating the Impact of Leadership Development: A Professional Guide.* Center for Creative Leadership.

2004. McCauley, C. D., Van Velsor, E. *The Center For Creative Leadership Handbook of Leadership Development* (2nd ed). Jossey-Bass.

2005. Bunker, K. A., & Wakefield, M. *Leading with Authenticity in Times of Transition.* Center for Creative Leadership.

2005. Hughes, R. L., & Beatty, K. C. *Becoming a Strategic Leader: Your Role in Your Organization's Enduring Success.* Jossey-Bass.

2006. Hannum, K., Martineau, J. W., & Reinelt, C. (Eds.). *The Handbook of Leadership Development Evaluation.* Jossey-Bass.

2006. Ting, S., & Scisco, P. (Eds.). *The CCL Handbook of Coaching: A Guide for the Leader Coach.* Jossey-Bass.

2007. Deal, J. J. *Retiring the Generation Gap: How Employees Young and Old can Find Common Ground.* Wiley.

2007. Drath, W. *The Deep Blue Sea: Rethinking the Source of Leadership.* Jossey-Bass.

2008. Bal, V., Campbell, M. J., & McDowell-Larsen, S. *Managing Leadership Stress.* Center for Creative Leadership.

2008. Drath, Wilfred H., Cynthia D. McCauley, Charles J. Palus, Ellen Van Velsor, Patricia M. G. O'Connor, and John B. McGuire. Direction, alignment, commitment: Toward a more integrative ontology of leadership. *The Leadership Quarterly* 19, no. 6 (2008): 635–53.

2008. Fleenor, J. W., Taylor, S., & Chappelow, C. *Leveraging the Impact of 360-degree Feedback.* Pfeiffer.

2009. Leslie, J.B., Chandrasekar, A., & Barts, D. *Leadership Gap Indicator Technical Manual.* Center for Creative Leadership.

2009. McGuire, J. B., & Rhodes, G. B. *Transforming Your Leadership Culture.* Jossey-Bass.

2010. Velsor, E. V., McCauley, C. D., & Ruderman, M. N. *The Center for Creative Leadership Handbook of Leadership Development* (3rd ed.). John Wiley & Sons.

2010. Wilson, M. S. *Developing Tomorrow's Leaders Today: Insights from Corporate India.* John Wiley & Sons (Asia).

2011. Ernst, C., & Chrobot-Mason, D. (2011). *Boundary Spanning Leadership: Six Practices for Solving Problems, Driving Innovation, and Transforming Organizations.* McGraw Hill.

2011. Hannum, K. M., Braddy, P. W., Leslie, J. B., Ruderman, M. N., & Kossek, E. E. *WorkLife Indicator: Increasing your Effectiveness On and Off the Job Technical Manual.* Center for Creative Leadership.

2011. Leslie, J. B., & Peterson, M. J. *The Benchmarks Sourcebook: Three Decades of Related Research.* Center for Creative Leadership.

2012. Campbell, D. *Campbell Leadership Indicator Facilitator Guide.* Center for Creative Leadership.

2013. Leslie, J. B. *Feedback to Managers: A Guide to Reviewing and Selecting Multirater Instruments for Leadership Development* (4th ed.). Center for Creative Leadership.

2013.   Ruderman, M. N., Braddy, P. W., Hannum, K. M., & Kossek, E. E. *Managing Your Whole Life*. Center for Creative Leadership.

2014.   Hughes, R. L., Beatty, K. C., & Dinwoodie, D. *Becoming a Strategic Leader: Your Role in Your Organization's Enduring Success* (2nd ed.). Jossey-Bass.

2014.   McCauley, C. D., DeRue, D. S., Yost, P. R., & Taylor, S. (Eds.). *Experience-Driven Leader Development: Models, Tools, Best Practices, and Advice for on-the-Job Development*. Wiley.

2014.   Palus, C. J., & Horth, D. M. *Visual Explorer*. Center for Creative Leadership.

2014.   Ruderman, M., Clerkin, C., & Connolly, C. *Leadership Development Beyond Competencies: Moving to a Holistic Approach*. Center for Creative Leadership.

2014.   Wilson, M. S. & Chandrasekar N. Anand. *Experience Explorer*. Center for Creative Leadership.

2015.   Passmore, B. *Leading Continuous Change: Navigating Churn in the Real World*. Berrett-Koehler

2015.   Riddle, D., Hoole, E. R., & Gullette, E. C. D. (Eds.). *The Center for Creative Leadership Handbook of Coaching In Organizations*. Jossey-Bass.

2016.   Cullen-Lester, K. L., & Yammarino, F. J. Collective and network approaches to leadership: Special issue introduction. *The Leadership Quarterly*, 27(2), 173–180.

2016.   Gentry, W. A. *Be the Boss Everyone Wants to Work For: A Guide for New Leaders*. Berrett-Koehler.

2017.   Center for Creative Leadership. *Boundary Spanning Leadership Workshop Facilitator Kit*. Center for Creative Leadership.

2017   Deal, J. J., & Levenson, A. R. *What Millennials Want from Work: How to Maximize Engagement in Today's Workforce*. McGraw Hill.

2016.   McDowell, S. *The Care and Feeding of the Leader's Brain*. Center for Creative Leadership.

2017.   McGuire, J. B., Palus J., Pasmore, W., & Rhodes, G.B. *Transforming Your Organization*. Center for Creative Leadership.

2017. Scisco, P., Biech, E., & Hallenbeck, G. *Compass: Your Guide for Leadership Development and Coaching.* Center for Creative Leadership.

2018. Center for Creative Leadership. *CCL Fusion.* Center for Creative Leadership.

2018. Leslie, J., & Hoole, E. *How to Lead Virtual Teams: The Power of Leveraging Polarities.* Center for Creative Leadership.

2018. Young, S., Champion, H., Stawiski, S., Smith, M., & Mondore, S. *Using Predictive Analytics to Drive More Effective Leadership Actions.* Center for Creative Leadership.

2018. Puri, S. *The Global Asian Leader: From Local Star to Global CXO.* Center for Creative Leadership.

2019. Center for Creative Leadership. *Team Vantage.* Center for Creative Leadership.

2019. Mehta, S., & Downs, H. *Six Strategies for Digital Learning Success.* Center for Creative Leadership.

2019 Puri, S., Chandrasekar, A., Shaik, F. B., & Abas, A. A. B. *Bold 3.0: Future-Fluent Board Leadership in Asia.* Center for Creative Leadership.

2019. Ruderman, M. N., & Clerkin, C. *The Quantified Leader: Wearables & Self-tracking Technology for Development.* Center for Creative Leadership.

2020. Fernandez, K., Clerkin, C., & Ruderman, M. N. (2020). *The Stories We Tell: Why Cognitive Distortions Matter For Leaders.* Center for Creative Leadership.

2020. Fleenor, J.W., Taylor, S., and Chappelow, C. *Leveraging the Impact of 360-degree Feedback* (2nd ed.). Berrett-Koehler.

2020. Leis, M., & Reinecke, S. *Social-Emotional Leadership: A Guide for Youth Development.* Center for Creative Leadership.

2020. Leslie, J. B. *Pandemic Paradoxes and How They Affect Your Workers.* Center for Creative Leadership.

2020. McCauley, C., & Fick-Cooper, L. *Direction, Alignment, Commitment: Achieving Better Results through Leadership (Second Edition).* Center for Creative Leadership.

2020.   Stawiski, S., Jeong, S., & Champion, H. *Leadership Development Impact (LDI) Framework*. Center for Creative Leadership.

2021.   Balakrishnan, R., Young, S., Leslie, J., McCauley, C., & Ruderman, M. *Leadership Challenger Ladder (LCL) Technical Report*. Center for Creative Leadership.

2021.   Ruderman, M. N., Clerkin, & Fernandez, K. C. *Resilience that Works: Eight Practices for Leadership and Life*. Center for Creative Leadership.

2021.   Truninger, M., Ruderman, M. N., Clerkin, C., Fernandez, K. C., & Cancro, D. Sounds like a Leader: An Ascription–actuality Approach to Examining Leader Emergence and Effectiveness. *The Leadership Quarterly*, 32(5), 101420.

2021.   Wormington, S., Nagarajan, L., & Chow-Paul, F. (Eds.). *ASEM Youth Report For Young People, By Young People: Insights into Young Adults' Leadership Experiences and Aspirations in ASEM Countries*. Asia-Europe Foundation and Center for Creative Leadership.

2022.   Anand, M. K., Chandrasekar, A., Chen, H., Mallis, E., Puri, S., & Chong, Y. T. *Work 3.0: Reimagining Leadership in a Hybrid World, Asia-Pacific Study*. Center for Creative Leadership.

2022.   Loignon, Andy, Stephanie Wormington, and George Hallenbeck. *Reconsidering Myths about Teamwork Using CCL's Framework on Team Effectiveness*. Center for Creative Leadership.

2022.   Ehrlich, V. A. *Leadership Development as a Lever for Social Change*. Center for Creative Leadership.

2022.   Kosovich, J. & Schneider, M. *Community Equity Indicator*. Center for Creative Leadership.

2022.   Puri, S., Chandrasekar, A., Mallis, E., & Looi. *The Global Asian Leader: From Asia, For the World*. Center for Creative Leadership.

2022.   Reinecke, S., & Leis, M. *Building Bridges: Leadership for You and Me*. Center for Creative Leadership.

2022.   Young, S., Diaz, J., DeCoutere, B., & Downs, H. *Leadership Development in the Flow of Work: Leveraging Technology to Accelerate Learning*. Center for Creative Leadership.

2023.   Bergeron, D. M. Monday mourning: A call for the study of bereavement in the workplace. *Journal of Management Inquiry.*

2023.   Dunne-Moses, A., Dawkins, M. A., Ehrlich, V. E., Clerkin, C., & Chelsea, C. *The Research Foundations for REAL: A Framework for Leadership Action in Equity, Diversity & Inclusion.* Center for Creative Leadership.

2023.   Fry, E. B., & Schneider, M. *Latinas Leading Change: A Case Study of Leadership Development for Community Impact.* Center for Creative Leadership.

2023.   Leslie, J. B., Peterson, M. J., & Fleenor, J. W. *The Benchmarks Sourcebook: Four Decades of Related Research.* Center for Creative Leadership.

About the Authors

Jean Brittain Leslie is a Senior Fellow and Director of Strategic Initiatives in CCL's Leadership Research & Analytics Group. In this role, she develops and implements programs, projects, and processes that support the group's vision and plans. With over 35 years at CCL, Jean has made significant contributions in research, publishing, product development, and training. She conducted some of CCL's first cross-cultural research projects and published the findings for practicing managers. Her interest in cultural issues led to her translating, adapting, and validating CCL assessments for international use.

Jean has also developed expertise in 360-degree feedback. She is a co-author of CCL's flagship 360 instrument Benchmarks and the Leadership Gap Indicator organizational assessment. She has served as an instructor for CCL's Assessment Certification Workshop and Emerging Leaders Program and has authored over 100 pieces on leadership, assessment, and feedback, including peer-reviewed articles, popular press articles, book chapters, and books.

Peter L. Scisco is an author, freelance writer, and book editor. He is co-author of CCL's *Change Now! 5 Steps to Better Leadership* and *Compass: Your Guide for Leadership Development and Coaching*. His work on organizational discourse appears in the *Handbook of Organizational Rhetoric and Communication: Foundations of Dialogue, Discourse, Narrative, and Engagement*. Peter has published in more than 200 periodicals across a broad array of subjects, including career development, personal technology, and interactive entertainment.

About the Center for Creative Leadership

At the Center for Creative Leadership, our drive to create a ripple effect of positive change underpins everything we do. For 50+ years, we've pioneered leadership development solutions for everyone from frontline workers to global CEOs. Consistently ranked among the world's top providers of executive education, our research-based programs and solutions inspire individuals in organizations across the world — including 2/3 of the Fortune 1000 — to ignite remarkable transformations.

www.ingramcontent.com/pod-product-compliance
Lightning Source LLC
Chambersburg PA
CBHW042119190326
41519CB00030B/7546